OXFORD
UNIVERSITY PRESS

Using a Computer

Chantelle Greenhills

Contents

A computer is a machine that helps people to use and exchange information. The information could include words, numbers, pictures or sounds. Television stations use computers to produce shows. Traffic lights are controlled by computers. Every day, your life will involve a computer in some way. But this was not always so.

A television station control room

Traffic lights

In 1931, this big calculating machine was used for counting millions of people.

A small modern calculator

People have always tried to invent machines to help them in their work. The first calculator was made in 1642. It could add and subtract numbers. This was the first step towards making a computer. But it did not use electricity.

The first computer that used electricity was made in 1945. It could store numbers and do about 300 sums every second.

This computer was very large. It filled two big rooms. Each day, it used the same amount of electricity as 10 family houses.

Some early computers were so big that just one filled a whole room.

This modern PC can fit on a desk.

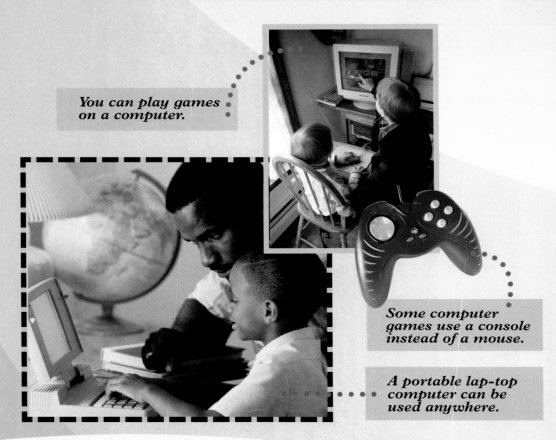

You can play games on a computer.

Some computer games use a console instead of a mouse.

A portable lap-top computer can be used anywhere.

Over the next 30 years, computers got smaller. In 1975, computers that could be used in people's homes went on sale. These were called 'personal computers' or PCs.

Computers are getting smaller and smaller, and better and better. They can be **programmed** to carry out many tasks at the same time.

There are now many different types of computers. Some are better for business and some for playing games.

Imagine your school wanted to tell everybody to come to a special event, such as a Big Book Sale. You would need some posters to tell them:
• what it is about;
• when it will happen;
• where to find it.

You might make the posters using paper, pens, rubbers, rulers, crayons or paints – and lots of helpers. Or you could make them much more quickly, using a computer with a printer and a connection to the **Internet**.

Writing the Words

Valley Junior School
Big Book Sale
Saturday 1st March
11 a.m.
in the
Scho

Click on the writing program icon.

Think about what you want to say. What information do people need to know?
What? When? Where?

To start making your poster, click on the writing program **icon** on your screen. Type in the words you want on the blank page.

If you change your mind, or make a mistake, it is easy to change things on a computer. You can 'rub out' words using the **delete** key, and type in different words.

Changing the Font

There are many ways of making the words in the text eye-catching.

You can change the way the letters in the text look by clicking the Font button. This will show you samples of letters in different fonts. Use the mouse to **highlight** the text. Then choose the font style you like by clicking on it.

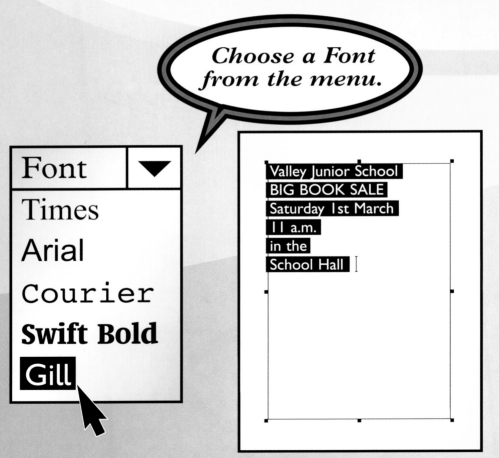

Choose a Font from the menu.

Font ▼

Times

Arial

Courier

Swift Bold

Gill

Valley Junior School
BIG BOOK SALE
Saturday 1st March
11 a.m.
in the
School Hall

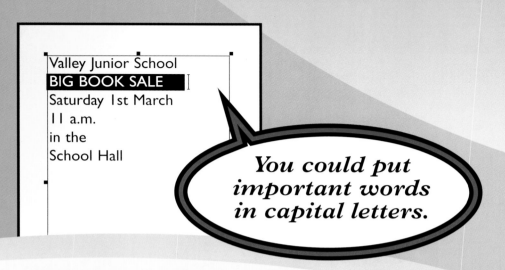

Valley Junior School
BIG BOOK SALE
Saturday 1st March
11 a.m.
in the
School Hall

You could put important words in capital letters.

Remember that some words like 'Saturday' should begin with a capital letter.

You might also like to write some important words with capitals for every letter. This will make people take more notice of them.

You could change the size of the letters, too, and the spacing between the lines.

You could change the size of the words.

Valley Junior School

BIG
BOOK
SALE

Saturday 1st March
11 a.m. in the School Hall

Arranging the Layout

You could change the position of the text. This is called the layout.

The text could be centred. This will spread the words out from the middle of the page. Or the lines could be arranged at one side or the other.

The computer can change this with one click. You do not have to write the words out again, as you would if you were using a pen.

You could change the position of the text.

Valley Junior School

BIG
BOOK SALE

Saturday 1st March
11 a.m. in the School Hall

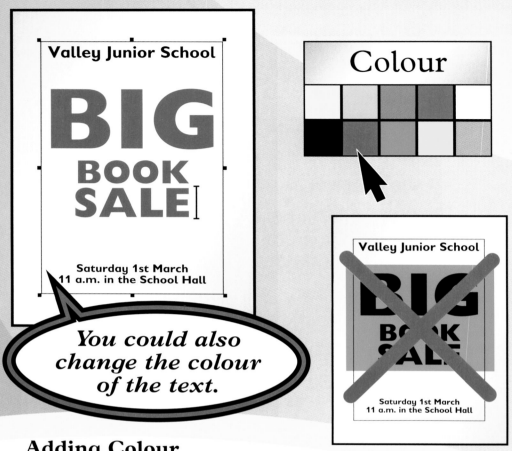

Adding Colour

You could also change the colour of the text if you have a colour button. Clicking this will show you samples of colours you can choose.

If you have a colour printer, you will be able to print your poster out in colour.

Avoid putting in large panels of colour, or your printer will quickly run out of ink, just like a coloured pen would.

Is It Easy to Read?

Make sure that all the words in the text are very clear and easy to read from a long way away. That is the secret of a good poster.

Valley Junior School

BIG
BOOK
SALE

**Saturday 1st March
11 a.m.
in the School Hall**

Valley Junior School

BIG
BOOK
SALE

Saturday 1st March
11 a.m.
in the School Hall

*Which poster
is easier to read?*

Putting in Pictures

Make your poster look really exciting by adding pictures.

If you like drawing, click on the drawing tool and draw your own picture. 'Copy' and 'Paste' it into your poster. If you don't know how to do this, ask for help. Your teacher or a friend could show you. There are also instructions on the Help menu on the tool bar.

Using Clip Art

Drawing by hand can take a long time. But with computers there is a quicker way.

You could find Clip Art in the **menu**, and add a piece of ready-made art to your poster.

Change the size or the colour of it if you want to.

Fish

Bicycle

Boy Jumping

Bookworm

Umbrella

Picture Preview

Find Clip Art in the menu.

Valley Junior School

BIG
BOOK
SALE

Saturday 1st March
11 a.m.
in the School Hall

Photographs

Does your school have a **scanner**? If it does, you can scan a photograph and copy and paste it into your poster. You could use a photograph of your school library, or of a group of children looking at books.

You might be able to take a photograph with a digital camera. The pictures from these cameras can be loaded straight onto a computer.

Using the Internet

Another place to find pictures is on the **Internet**. If your computer has an Internet connection, look for 'Book Sale' pictures. Ask your teacher to help you to find the right **website**. Copy one onto your poster.

Adding a Border

Add a border to frame your poster.

It is easy to move pictures around on the computer screen. Arrange all the pictures or photographs around the text. Then add a border to frame your poster. Your computer will probably have several tools to help you do this. You can choose from borders with different lines or patterns.

When you have finished designing your poster, check all the words and pictures.

Make sure all the information is correct and nothing is missing. It is easy to **delete** things by accident on a computer.

You could use the Spell Check tool to check the spelling.

Now save your work. Give it a title you can remember easily.

Spell Check

Suspect word: 'a.m.'

am
aim
a
an

[Skip] [Ignore] [Replace]

Replace with:

Valley Junior School

BIG
BOOK
SALE

Saturday 1st March
11 a.m.
in the School Hall

Now save your work.

Print out one copy of your poster first so that you can check it. Ask a friend or your teacher to check it, too.

When you are sure everything is right, print out lots of copies of your poster. Pin them up where everyone can see them.

You could post copies of your poster to friends, or to another school. But with a computer you can send them even faster, by e-mail.

Open a new e-mail and type in the e-mail addresses of the people you want to send them to. Type in a message. Then **insert** the file that you saved with your poster in it.

Insert the file with your poster on it.

To: m.jones@daydream.co.uk

Hi Melanie
We are having a BIG book sale at my school. I have attached my poster for you to see. Please pin it up in your school.
From Stephen

21

Good Uses for Computers

As well as making posters, there are hundreds of ways you could use a computer. Here are just some:
- making greetings cards;
- writing homework;
- drawing and labelling diagrams;
- doing research for projects on the **Internet**;
- writing letters;
- sending messages by e-mail.

What others can you think of?

delete – To rub out or remove.

icon – A small symbol or picture on the computer screen. If you click on the icon it opens a program or window.

insert – To put something into another thing.

Internet – An international computer network that allows people to get information from lots of computers.

highlight – To make something show up clearly.

menu – A list of things to choose from.

program – A list of instructions put into a computer to tell it what to do. A games computer is **programmed** to play games.

scanner – A machine that can copy pictures onto your computer.

website – A page on the Internet that you can look at on your computer.

Index